SPECIAL OPERATIONS WINGS

by Tracey Boraas

Special thanks to
U.S. Air Force 16th Special Operations Wings
Public Affairs Office
Hurlburt Field, Florida

CAPSTONE BOOKS

an imprint of Capstone Press
Mankato, Minnesota

Capstone Books are published by Capstone Press
151 Good Counsel Drive, P. O. Box 669, Mankato, Minnesota 56002
http://www.capstone-press.com

Library of Congress Cataloging-in-Publication Data
Boraas, Tracey.
    U.S. Air Force Special Forces: Special Operations Wings/by Tracey Boraas.
    p. cm.—(Warfare and weapons)
    Includes bibliographical references (p. 45) and index.
    Summary: Introduces the United States Air Force's Special Operations Wings
including their history, development, missions, specific jobs of crewmembers,
and equipment.
    ISBN 0-7368-0336-X
    1. United States—Air Forces—Juvenile literature. 2. Special operations
(Military science)—Juvenile literature. 3. Special forces (Military science)—United
States—Juvenile literature. [1. United States—Air Forces. 2. Special operations
(Military science) 3. Special forces (Military science)] I. Title. II. Title: U.S. Air
Force Special Forces. III. Series.
UG633.B67   2000
358.4—dc21   99-25470
                                                                                            CIP

Editorial Credits
Blake Hoena, editor; Timothy Halldin, cover designer; Linda Clavel, illustrator;
    Heidi Schoof, photo researcher

Photo Credits
Bohrer, David, cover
Corbis/Aero Graphics, Inc., 33
Corbis/Bettmann, 17, 19
Corbis/Hulton-Deutsche Collection, 14
Defense Visual Information Center; 4, 6, 9, 11, 20, 24, 27, 30, 35, 37, 40, 43

**Special thanks to David Bohrer, Pulitzer Prize-winning photographer for the
Los Angeles Times, for providing the cover photo.**

Table of Contents

Chapter 1

Special Operations Wings

On January 8, 1998, two men overturned their raft on the French Broad River in North Carolina. The men had been rafting through an 800-foot (244-meter) deep canyon at the time. One man held onto the overturned raft and was carried safely downstream. The other man remained trapped in the canyon. He clung to a tree that hung over the river to keep from drowning.

A witness contacted the Madison County Emergency Center about the man in trouble. But it was getting dark and raining very hard. This would make a rescue attempt difficult.

16th SOW members used MH-53J Pave Low helicopters during the French Broad River rescue.

SOW units may deliver food and supplies for the U.S. military to hand out to people in need.

Nearby, members of the 16th Special Operations Wing (16th SOW) were performing training exercises. The 16th SOW members were flying two MH-53J Pave Low helicopters. Authorities at the Madison County Emergency Center contacted these 16th SOW members for help with the rescue.

The 16th SOW members quickly flew to the man in trouble. One helicopter shined a light on the man as the other helicopter lowered a hoist to him. The 16th SOW members lifted him into the helicopter with this cable. They then flew him to safety.

"Any Time, Any Place"
Special Operations Wing units are specially trained members of the U.S. Air Force (USAF). They train for missions that regular USAF units may not be able to perform.

SOW units' duties often involve high-risk and immediate-action assignments. SOW units must be prepared for duty at all times. Also, their missions often are secretive and dangerous. These missions may involve combat. They may involve gathering information about enemy forces. SOW units also may try to rescue hostages. These prisoners are held against their will. SOW units even may bring food to people living in war zones.

SOW units train to be prepared for any situation. They have a motto for the duties they perform. Their saying is "Any Time, Any Place."

The 16th Special Operations Wing

The USAF has three active wing units that perform similar duties. Members of these units work for the USAF full time. These units use military aircraft to perform their missions. The 16th Special Operations Wing is one such unit. It is based at Hurlburt Field, Florida.

The 16th SOW is the oldest, largest, and most experienced wing unit. The 16th SOW has more than 7,000 members and more than 70 aircraft. The 16th SOW has existed since World War II (1939–1945). This unit has had several different names such as 1st Air Commando Group and 1st SOW. In 1993, the USAF changed the unit's name to the 16th SOW.

The 16th SOW is part of the Air Force Special Operations Command (AFSOC). The AFSOC is part of the U.S. Special Operations Command (USSOCOM). USSOCOM also includes units from the army, navy, and marines. Units assigned to USSOCOM are responsible for covert operations. These secret missions often are dangerous and take special training to perform.

SOW units use aircraft to perform their missions.

The 16th SOW performs many types of covert operations. For these missions, they may fly troops into hostile territory. The 16th SOW often performs missions at night and in poor weather. These conditions make it more difficult for enemy troops to spot 16th SOW aircraft. The 16th SOW may be ordered to drop supplies to U.S. troops in enemy territory. They also may fly injured troops out of enemy territory.

The 16th SOW takes part in psychological operations. These missions attempt to change the thinking and behavior of people in hostile areas. The 16th SOW drops leaflets in areas where people oppose U.S. interests. These letters tell people about U.S. views. The U.S. government uses leaflets to convince people to support its views and interests.

Other Air Force Special Operations Units
The 352nd Special Operations Group (SOG) is another active wing unit in the USAF. The 352nd SOG is located at the Royal Air Force Base in Mildenhall, England. Members of this unit perform special operations missions in Europe, Africa, and the Middle East. These missions are similar to those performed by the 16th Special Operations Wing. They also may involve working with allied forces. These military forces are from countries friendly to the United States.

The 353rd SOG is the third active wing unit. This group is located at Kadena Air Base in Japan. Members of this unit perform special

The 193rd SOW airplanes are equipped for radio and television broadcast.

operations in the Pacific Ocean region. During peacetime, the 353rd SOG prepares for combat. It trains and practices military drills throughout the Pacific region.

National Guard and Reserve Units

The 193rd Special Operations Wing unit is an Air Force National Guard unit. Most of the members in this unit do not work full time for the USAF. They train only for a few days each month. The 193rd SOW is based at Harrisburg International Airport in Middletown, Pennsylvania.

The 193rd SOW provides airborne radio and television broadcasts. This unit has several specially equipped airplanes that can transmit these broadcasts. The 193rd SOW sometimes uses these aircraft to help people during emergencies such as earthquakes, tornadoes, or floods. These emergencies may be in the United States or other countries. The 193rd SOW uses radio and television broadcasts to tell people what to do during these emergencies.

The 919th SOW is a reserve unit. Members of this unit are not on active duty. They do not work for the USAF full time. Instead, they train for a few days each month. But 919th members may be called to perform missions during wars. The 919th SOW is based at Duke Field, Florida.

Winged silver dagger: stands for the mission of air commandos

Blue: represents the sky and the U.S. Air Force

ANY TIME ANY PLACE

Red and white stripes: represent the original air commandos of World War II

Golden lamp: stands for the knowledge and help the 16th SOW provides to people around the world

Chapter 2

History

During World War II, Japan attacked several countries in Asia. These countries included China, Burma, and India. British troops tried to protect these countries from the Japanese. The U.S. military wanted to support the British troops.

At the time, the U.S. military did not have a separate branch for the air force. Instead, the air force was part of the army and called the Army Air Forces (AAF). In August 1943, the AAF developed Project 9 to support British troops fighting the Japanese. The soldiers who trained to perform this mission were called air commandos.

These British troops were fighting the Japanese in the jungles of Burma during World War II.

15

Air Commandos

Air commandos flew many difficult and dangerous missions into Japanese-held territory. Air commandos flew many of their missions at night. They used only navigational instruments to guide their aircraft. These instruments showed how high and fast they were flying their aircraft.

Air commandos landed in jungle areas to drop off troops and supplies. During World War II, they flew almost 10,000 British troops into Japanese-held territory. They also brought nearly 250 tons (227 metric tons) of supplies to these troops.

Air commandos also performed other duties. They blew up enemy bridges and railroads. They attacked enemy troops. They fought in air-to-air combat with enemy aircraft. They even transported all the dead, wounded, and sick soldiers from enemy territory. This was the first time in military history that this was possible.

World War II marked a turning point for air power. The air commandos' support helped

World War II ended in 1945 after the Japanese surrendered to the United States.

British forces succeed against Japanese forces. Now the U.S. military was able to fly troops and supplies into enemy territory. In March 1944, the AAF named this group of air commandos the 1st Air Commando Group.

World War II ended in 1945. That same year, the 1st Air Commando Group was ordered out of action. In 1947, the AAF became a separate part of the U.S. military. It was named the United States Air Force. The USAF eliminated the 1st Air Commando Group in October 1948. The USAF did not need this group during peacetime.

Rebirth of the Air Commandos

In 1961, President John F. Kennedy ordered the military to start training airborne warfare specialists. The USAF then developed new air commando units. These units were sent to help U.S. and South Vietnamese troops in the Vietnam War (1954–1975). Air commandos flew troops in and out of the Vietnamese jungles.

In 1963, these air commando units were renamed the 1st Air Commando Wing (1st ACW). In 1968, the USAF changed the name of the 1st ACW to 1st Special Operations Wing. Since then, the 1st SOW has performed many military operations.

Since the Vietnam War

In 1980, the 1st Special Operations Wing took part in Operation Eagle Claw. Members of the 1st SOW tried to help rescue American hostages held

In 1961, President John F. Kennedy ordered the military to train airborne warfare specialists.

in Iran. But the rescue attempt failed. Five 1st SOW members died when their helicopter crashed.

In 1983, the 1st SOW assisted a drug task force in southern Florida. The 1st SOW's job was to stop people from bringing illegal drugs into the United States. The 1st SOW helped capture and destroy $1.5 billion in illegal drugs, vehicles, equipment, and weapons. These items belonged to drug dealers.

SOW members helped bomb Iraqi military targets during the Gulf War.

In 1983, members of the 1st SOW took part in Operation Urgent Fury. They joined forces with the army, navy, and marines. During this mission, the United States sent troops to protect U.S. medical students in Grenada. Rebels had taken over the government on this Caribbean island. The U.S. government believed these people might harm the medical students.

The 1st SOW took part in Operation Just Cause in 1989. This mission took place in

Panama. General Manuel Noriega was using his military force to keep power in Panama. He kept the elected government out of power there. 1st SOW members helped capture Noriega and defeat his military force.

In 1991, 1st SOW units took part in Operation Desert Storm. The government of Iraq had sent troops into Kuwait. Operation Desert Storm was meant to drive these troops from Kuwait. 1st SOW units dropped leaflets into Iraq from aircraft. Leaflets told the Iraqi people how the United States wanted to improve their living conditions. The 1st SOW also dropped bombs in combat. They performed a combat search-and-rescue mission. This mission rescued a navy pilot whose aircraft had been shot down by enemy fire.

In 1992 and 1993, the 1st SOW flew missions during operations Restore Hope and Continue Hope. The United States sent troops to Somalia for these missions. The troops tried to keep peace and help supply food to starving citizens in this African country.

In 1993, the USAF renamed the 1st SOW. This unit now was called the 16th SOW.

Mission

Operation: Eagle Claw

Date: April 24, 1980

Location: Tehran, Iran

Situation: Iranian students took U.S. citizens hostage.

Mission: Members of the 1st SOW were assigned to transport by helicopter special forces units to Tehran. These special forces would rescue the hostages. They included U.S. Army Rangers and U.S. Air Force Combat Controllers.

Fatal Crash: The helicopters needed to be refueled during the mission. At a location inside of Iran, C-130 tanker planes would refuel the helicopters while in flight. During the refueling, one of the C-130 planes crashed into one of the helicopters. Five 1st SOW members died in the crash. Three other U.S. soldiers also died.

Mission's end: The mission was called off after the crash. There were no longer enough helicopters to carry the soldiers and hostages. The U.S. military decided after this mission that it needed better trained special forces units. The army's Nightstalkers were one group developed after Operation Eagle Claw. Nightstalkers train to fly helicopters during special operations missions.

ARMENIA

TURKEY

IRAQ

SAUDI
ARABIA

Chapter 3

On the Job

Each Special Operations Wing unit has many crewmembers. Each crewmember performs a certain job. But the crewmembers must work well together as a team. The success of their missions often depends on teamwork.

Becoming an Officer

All members of the USAF are called airmen. Some airmen train to be officers.

There are several ways to become an officer. Airmen can attend the Air Force Academy in Colorado Springs, Colorado, to become an officer. They also can become an officer by entering the Reserve Officer Training Corps (ROTC) while in college. Airmen who do not go to the Air Force Academy or join ROTC can still

Airmen can become officers by attending the Air Force Academy in Colorado Springs.

become an officer. They need to earn a college degree and then attend officer training school.

Officers
Each aircraft crew has a pilot and a co-pilot. The co-pilot helps the pilot fly the aircraft. These pilots are officers. Special Operations Wing pilots learn to fly one type of aircraft. Pilots may learn to fly helicopters, gunships, or tanker aircraft. Tanker aircraft refuel other aircraft in flight.

Each crew also has a navigator. The navigator reports to the pilot. The navigator and pilot work together to keep the aircraft flying safely. The navigator reads instruments that tell how the aircraft is moving. The instruments help the navigator direct the flight of the aircraft. The navigator makes sure the aircraft follows a safe course.

An Electronic Warfare Officer (EWO) helps protect the aircraft and its crewmembers. The EWO uses electronic equipment to watch for enemy forces. Enemy troops or aircraft may try to shoot down the aircraft. The EWO uses the aircraft's defense systems to protect the aircraft.

Aerial gunners make sure the weapons aboard SOW aircraft are loaded correctly.

Gunships have Fire Control Officers (FCOs). FCOs control the weapons aboard gunships. These officers direct the aircraft weapons' fire at enemy targets.

Non-Officers
Some airmen are enlisted members of the USAF. These airmen do not train to become officers. Enlisted members of Special

Operations Wing units also have specific duties to perform.

Aerial gunners are enlisted airmen. They load weapons with bullets. Aerial gunners make sure the weapons are loaded and fire correctly. Weapons will not fire if they are loaded incorrectly.

Some enlisted airmen in SOW units are flight engineers. Flight engineers oversee the mechanical operations of aircraft while in flight. Flight engineers make sure aircraft are operating properly.

Loadmasters also are enlisted airmen. They check the weight and balance of the cargo aircraft carry. Loadmasters make sure aircraft will be able to fly safely while carrying a large amount of weight.

Some aircrews include sensor operators. These enlisted airmen search for enemy targets using equipment aboard their aircraft.

Military Terms

AAF – Army Air Forces

AFB – Air Force Base

AFSOC – Air Force Special Operations Command

EWO – Electronic Warfare Officer

FCO – Fire Control Officer

friendly – U.S. or allied troops

Hooyah – a word spoken by a person who agrees with what someone is saying

hostile – enemy troops

hot spot – a country or region where a dangerous situation such as a war may exist or start

Rainbows – airmen arriving at basic training in brightly colored civilian clothing

ROTC – Reserve Officer Training Corps

rotor heads – helicopter pilots

SOG – Special Operations Group

USSOCOM – U.S. Special Operations Command

Chapter 4

Aircraft and Equipment

Special Operations Wing units use a variety of aircraft. Each type of aircraft has special equipment. Some aircraft have weapons for combat. Some have rescue equipment. Others have air-to-air refueling equipment. This equipment is used to refuel other aircraft while flying.

Each type of aircraft flies differently. Some aircraft can fly high above the ground and at high speeds. Others are built to fly close to the ground. Different types of aircraft work better for different types of missions.

SOW units use aircraft to perform their missions.

Gunships

The USAF has used the AC-130H Spectre Gunship since the Vietnam War. This airplane is armed with heavy artillery. It has several large guns mounted to its sides.

The AC-130H also has a sensor system. This system uses radar, a TV sensor, and an infrared sensor. These instruments use radio and light waves to locate troops and targets. This equipment also allows the AC-130H's crew to tell the difference between friendly and hostile forces on the ground. Gunships are used to protect friendly ground troops from enemy troops.

The AC-130U Gunship is the newest aircraft used by SOW units. This aircraft has been in use since 1995. It can be refueled while in flight. It also has several weapons mounted to its sides.

The AC-130U's sensor system is more advanced than the AC-130H model's system. The AC-130U can attack more than one long-range target at the same time.

Spectre Gunships use flares to confuse enemy missiles.

The AC-130U also has a defense system to protect itself. This system is similar to the one used on the AC-130H. It sends out flares. These bursts of bright light confuse enemy radar and sensor systems. This can help protect aircraft from enemy missile attacks.

Combat Talons

The Combat Talon is an airplane used to airdrop troops and equipment by parachute.

The Combat Talon can be flown in bad weather and at night. It also can be flown close to the ground. Combat Talons have an air-to-air refueling system.

SOW units have used the MC-130H Combat Talon II since 1991. This airplane is similar to the Talon I, but it is more automated. Machines perform some of the operations aboard this aircraft. This reduces the crew size. The Combat Talon I needs nine crewmembers. The Talon II needs only seven crewmembers.

Combat Shadow

Special Operations Wing units use the MC-130P Combat Shadow to refuel helicopters in flight. This aircraft also can be used to airdrop small special operations teams or supplies in enemy territory. SOW uses the Combat Shadow for secret missions. It is designed to be flown close to the ground and at night. This aircraft can be flown without outside lights. The Combat

The Combat Shadow can be equipped to refuel other aircraft in flight.

Shadow's crew uses night vision goggles. These goggles use light from the stars and the moon to help crewmembers see.

The Combat Shadow has been used since 1986. An improved version of this airplane is being designed. It will have a global positioning system. This system uses a satellite to help the crew track the airplane's location anywhere on Earth. Satellites are spacecraft orbiting the Earth. The Combat Shadow also will have a radar and missile warning system. This system warns crewmembers when they are being attacked.

Helicopters

Special Operations Wing units use two types of helicopters. SOW units use the MH-60G Pave Hawk mainly to transport troops in and out of war zones. This aircraft also can carry supplies for troops. The MH-60G works well for search-and-rescue missions in war zones. The MH-60G has a hoist to lift troops or equipment into the helicopter. The MH-60G can carry eight to 10 passengers.

The MH-60G helicopter also has an in-flight refueling probe. This pipe-like device connects the MH-60G with a tanker aircraft. An MH-60G can receive fuel from a tanker aircraft through this probe.

The MH-53J Pave Low III is the largest and most powerful helicopter SOW units use. This helicopter can fly troops in and out of war

The MH-60G Pave Hawk mainly is used to carry troops in and out of war zones.

zones. The MH-53J is equipped with armor plating. These metal plates protect the helicopter from enemy fire.

The MH-53J can carry 38 troops or 14 stretchers. These stretchers are used to carry injured troops to safety. The MH-53J also has a cargo hook that can carry 20,000 pounds (9,072 kilograms) outside the aircraft.

The MH-53J is one of the most advanced helicopters in the world. It has an advanced radar and map display system. The crew uses this system to avoid objects and to follow the ground. This allows pilots to fly the MH-53J close to the ground.

The CV-22 Osprey

The CV-22 Osprey is a tilt-rotor aircraft. This type of aircraft can take off and land in a small area just as a helicopter can. But the CV-22 Osprey also can fly like an airplane. It can fly farther and faster than most helicopters.

The CV-22 Osprey is an aircraft of the future. It will be used to take forces in and out of war zones. Beginning in 2004, the air force plans to replace the Pave Low helicopter with the CV-22 Osprey.

Important Dates

1939 – World War II begins

1943 – AAF trains air commandos for Project 9

1947 – Air force becomes a separate branch of the military

1954 – Vietnam War begins; military develops the AC-47, AC-119, and the AC-130 Gunships.

1961 – President John F. Kennedy orders the military to start training airborne warfare specialists

1966 – MC-130E Combat Talon I first used

1972 – AC-130H Spectre Gunship first used

1980 – Operation Eagle Claw; five 1st SOW members die in failed rescue attempt of U.S. hostages.

1981 – MH-53J Pave Low III first used

1982 – MH-60G Pave Hawk first used

1986 – MC-130P Combat Shadow first used

1991 – MC-130H Combat Talon II first used

1993 – USAF renames 1st SOW the 16th SOW

1995 – AC-130U Spectre Gunship first used

Chapter 5

Now and into the Future

Special Operations Wing units help people during peacetime. They rescue people in disaster areas. SOW members also perform search-and-rescue missions to find missing people. They may perform these missions in the United States or in other countries.

SOW units can be assigned to provide relief to suffering people around the world. SOW units may bring food and other basic supplies to these people. The 16th SOW has performed missions in Haiti, the Balkans, Somalia, and Liberia. They also helped Kurdish refugees in Turkey and northern Iraq

The U.S. military helped provide food to starving citizens in Somalia.

during Operation Provide Comfort. In Iraq, the 16th SOW helped provide food for starving citizens caught in war zones.

Current Missions

Currently, some Special Operations Wings units help support the North Atlantic Treaty Organization (NATO). Two 16th SOW units are helping U.S. and NATO troops keep peace in the Bosnia-Herzegovina region of Europe. These troops observe and gather information about this area. They also help make sure the people living in the Bosnia-Herzegovina region are not fighting.

The United States and Iraq have been in conflict throughout the 1990s. The 16th SOW has units stationed in the Persian Gulf in case greater conflict arises.

The Future

Situations continue to arise around the world that require special military attention. Special

SOW members are ready to travel anywhere in the world to perform missions.

units such as the 16th Special Operations Wing are trained to help meet these needs. They are ready for short-notice missions anywhere in the world.

Words to Know

airdrop (AIR-drop)—to drop troops or supplies by parachute from an aircraft

allies (AL-eyes)—people or groups that join together for a common cause

altitude (AL-ti-tood)—the height of an object above the ground

artillery (ar-TIL-uh-ree)—large, powerful guns

combat (KOM-bat)—fighting between people or armies

hostages (HOSS-tij-is)—people taken and held prisoner against their will

leaflet (LEEF-lit)—letters used to inform; the 16th SOW drops leaflets in hostile areas to inform people of U.S. views.

navigator (NAV-uh-gate-ur)—a person who helps the pilot direct the flight of an aircraft

radar (RAY-dar)—machinery that uses radio waves to locate objects and guide aircraft

To Learn More

Blue, Rose and Corinne J. Naden. *The U.S. Air Force*. Defending Our Country. Brookfield, Conn.: Millbrook Press, 1993.

Ferrell, Nancy Warren. *The U.S. Air Force*. Armed Service Series. Minneapolis: Lerner Publications Company, 1990.

Green, Michael. *The United States Air Force*. Serving Your Country. Mankato, Minn.: Capstone High/Low Books, 1998.

Useful Addresses

Air Force Historical Research Agency
600 Chennault Circle
Maxwell AFB, AL 36112-6424

Air Force Public Affairs Office
1690 Air Force Pentagon
Washington, DC 20330-1690

Hurlburt Field
16th Special Operations Wing/PA
131 Bartley Street
Suite 326
Hurlburt Field, FL 32544-527

United States Air Force Museum
1100 Spaatz Street
Wright-Patterson AFB, OH 45433-7102

Internet Sites

Air Force Images
http://www.af.mil/photos

Air Force Link Jr.
http://www.af.mil/aflinkjr

Air Force Special Operations Command
http://www.afsoc.af.mil

Commando Link
http://www.hurlburt.af.mil

Index